Clydebank – *Then a*

By John Hood

Text © John Hood, 2018.
First published in the United Kingdom, 2018,
by Stenlake Publishing Ltd.
Telephone: 01290 551122
www.stenlake.co.uk

ISBN 9781840338270

Printed by
Blissetts, Unit 1 Shield Drive,
West Cross Industrial Park, Brentford, TW8 9EX

Acknowledgements

I would particularly like to thank local historian and photographer Sam Gibson for undertaking the task of capturing the present-day scenes. I would also like to thank Mary Frances McGlynn, Local Studies and Reference Assistant, West Dunbartonshire Libraries, for her help in answering my many enquiries. The publishers would like to thank West Dunbartonshire Libraries, William Duncan, Bill Smith, Joan Trew, and the family of the late Jack Carson for their permission to reproduce photographs for this book.

Previous page and above: In the late 1970s the old tenement block in Chalmers Street, which for many years housed Clydebank's main post office, was demolished. It was subsequently replaced with a modern brick-built development comprising a newsagent, bookmaker, nightclub and fitness studio. Clydebank Co-operative's Central Drapery store, seen to the left of both photos, was formally opened in March 1917. Built in Renaissance style, it comprised a four-storey central block and lower west wing; at the time it was said to be the tallest commercial building in Clydebank. An identical east wing (seen in the present-day photo to the right of the central block) was later added. Also demolished in the late 1970s were tenements which stood opposite the Post Office; this was to enable the construction of Phase 1 of the new shopping centre. The small square-looking brick structure to the extreme left of the present-day photo, partially blocking the view of the Central Drapery, marks the beginning of the Phase 1 units, which included a modern post office facility. Missing from today's scene is the former Co-operative Creamery, which used to be adjacent to the east wing. The Creamery was opened in 1925 and closed in May 1982. It then lay derelict for a period until its demolition.

Introduction

Prior to the establishment of J. & G. Thomson's Clydebank shipyard at West Barns O' Clyde in 1871, the district, then known simply as Dalmuir, largely comprised open farmland with some cottages, the occasional turnpike road toll house and a few canal lock keepers' cottages. As a consequence, initially the vast majority of the new shipyard's workforce had to travel into Clydebank on a daily basis. However, it was felt that housing should be provided for these workers and the company therefore had two tenement blocks erected alongside the main gate of the shipyard. As the workforce steadily increased, further tenements were erected, almost all in close proximity to the shipyard. The establishment of yet another shipyard in 1887, on this occasion at East Barns O' Clyde, prompted more tenement construction, this time in the east end of the district. By the late 1880s, shortly after burgh status was achieved, an almost unbroken line of tenement buildings lined much of what would later become Dumbarton Road and Glasgow Road. At the same time side streets (e.g. Belmont Street, Alexander Street and Hume Street), running off at right angles to these two roads, were being laid out.

With the coming to Clydebank of the Kilbowie Iron Works in 1891 more tenements were erected on and around Kilbowie Road, in what would become Livingstone Street, Graham Street and Gordon Street. Frequently these tenements were constructed by or for the shipyard by private contractors, with factors employed to collect the rents on behalf of the landlords. Coinciding with the upsurge in tenement construction was the erection of other house types such as villas (for the professional and commercial classes) and cottages (for managers). In addition, schools, churches and shops were also erected.

Despite the establishment of the Singer Manufacturing Company on a 'greenfield' site at Kilbowie in 1882, the north of the district was initially little developed, although the company employed thousands from the outset. In fact, in contrast to the shipyard owners, Singer's only direct involvement in the provision of housing for their workers was the construction of a single tenement block (Singer Terrace) beside the Forth & Clyde Canal. The presence of Singer did, however, encourage a wave of speculative building from about 1885 onwards in an area on top of Kilbowie Hill, known locally as the Skypes. Again, while tenements predominated, other house types, such as villas, were built for those who could better afford them.

This house building continued into the 20th Century – for example, between 1906 and 1910 a total of 1,700 houses were erected. The growth in housing, facilities, and factories (and, as a consequence, population) led to Clydebank being commonly referred to as the 'risingest burgh'. Sadly, this success was cruelly brought to a halt in March 1941, during what became known as the Clydebank Blitz, when the burgh endured two evenings of Luftwaffe raids which killed over 600 people. Whole swathes of the district were left desolate; in addition to the loss of many schools and churches, over 43% of the council's housing stock was completely destroyed. Inevitably, due to wartime restrictions, and despite several post-war regeneration plans, the progress of re-building the shattered burgh was slow and was not finally completed until the early 1960s. However, outwith the old burgh area several post-war housing schemes were constructed at Whitecrook, Mountblow and Drumry, adding a total of 5,895 new houses to the burgh's housing stock. Sadly, this was followed with the decline throughout the 1960s and 1970s of the burgh's two principal industries (shipbuilding and sewing machines), resulting eventually in closures with substantial job losses.

The first of these losses came when the former John Brown Shipyard (by then part of the Upper Clyde Shipbuilders group, or UCS) closed in July 1971. This was followed in 1980 by the Singer Factory. Despite the closure of UCS, the shipyard did later operate as, firstly, the American Marathon Oil Company and, secondly, the French-owned Union Industrielle et d'Enterprise (UIE), both manufacturing oil rigs. The manufacture of gas turbines, firstly by John Brown Engineering (JBE), and latterly by its successor Kvaerner Energy, provided further employment within the shipyard and at Whitecrook and Rothesay Dock until 2001 (the shipyard site was then acquired by Clydeside Regeneration Limited).

On a more positive note, the loss of Clydebank's traditional industries did ultimately lead to Clydebank being chosen as the site for Scotland's first (and only) Enterprise Zone. Following its launch in August 1981, and the subsequent creation of a Scottish Development Agency (SDA) Task Force, funding was made available to regenerate the area. This led to the opening of Clydebank Business Park amongst other initiatives. In more recent years the work of regeneration has been continued by agencies such as Clydebank Re-built Limited and several local housing associations. Presently, the focus of these agencies has been to re-develop the riverside, encompassing both the Clydebank shipyard site and the site of the old Naval Construction Yard further down river at Dalmuir.

This 1930s' view shows the area around the Town Hall, looking west from Bruce Street. At that time, three-storey tenements lined both sides of Dumbarton Road as far as the 'Caley' bridge, which can just about be distinguished in the far distance beyond a Glasgow Corporation tram. The four-faced clock on the Town Hall bell tower was installed in 1930 and formed part of the Clydebank War Memorial. Just beyond the bell tower is the Morison Memorial Evangelical Union Church. Adjacent to the church is the classical-style Public Library, opened in 1910. This was quickly followed by the erection of more tenements to the west of the library. These tenements, known locally as the John Brown Buildings, were built around 1916 by Messrs John Brown & Company for their workers. The tenements were damaged during the Clydebank Blitz of March 1941, and in some cases were actually razed to the ground, leaving two large 'gap sites'. However, with the demise of UCS (the then owners of the tenements) in 1972, the tenements and gap sites were acquired by the Town Council, which subsequently initiated two 'new build' projects, carried out respectively by the World of Property Trust and Clydebank Housing Association in the late 1980s. This saw new housing built in the gap sites, in keeping with the style of the existing tenements, so that today the view on the left-hand side of this photograph appears virtually unchanged whereas, in complete contrast, the opposite side of Dumbarton Road is now devoid of all its tenements.

In this 1960s' view of Dumbarton Road looking west, the Town Hall bell tower casts its shadow on the tenements to the right of the picture. Although the two blocks of tenements appear largely intact, the exposed gable end and gap site of the Brandon Place tenements (at the junction with Miller Street, the first opening on the right) are a further reminder of the grim effects of the Clydebank Blitz. Beyond the Brandon Place tenements can be seen the Masonic Temple. All of these tenements were demolished in the 1970s as part of a burgh-wide slum clearance scheme. Later, a modern office block was erected at the near corner of Miller Street, on the site of McGowan & Cameron's Burgh Bar, with the area adjacent being landscaped to form Solidarity Plaza. From around 1971 until the 1980s, the site of the Brandon Place tenements was used as car parking for the Public Library opposite. At that time a suite of modern offices and shops was erected. These properties presently include the SixtyAteBar, which operated as Whisky Joe's from 1990 until 2003, when it became Singers, remaining so until recently. Still standing is the red sandstone Masonic Temple. Since it was vacated by the Lodge in 1965 the building has had various uses, including being a venue for Tim McMahon's Q4 and Oasis nightclubs. At the time of writing it was lying derelict.

On 4 February 1888 the rather grand-looking Clydebank Public School (the rear elevation of which is seen here) was opened by Sir John Neilston Cuthbertson, Chairman of Glasgow School Board. It replaced an earlier school on the site which, within ten years of its erection, had outgrown its pupil capacity. In this view the school is flanked on the left by the Rosebery Place tenement and on the right by properties on Kilbowie Road. Just glimpsed between the tenement and the school is Clydebank West Church. In 1911 the open space in the foreground was cleared for the construction of a new higher grade school, the main entrance of which was in Miller Street. Unlike the public school, the higher grade school survived the Clydebank Blitz, but in 1947 was vacated when the new Clydebank High School in Janetta Street was officially opened. Thereafter, it was used for, among other purposes, evening classes, but was finally demolished around 1983. Today, the site of both schools is occupied by modern office blocks opened in the 1990s.

On 6 September 1962, one week after Glasgow's tramway services were withdrawn, Clydebank held its own 'last caur' ceremony to mark the end of tramway services through the burgh. On that occasion, a Glasgow Corporation No. 9 Coronation Mark 1 tram, driven part of the way by Provost Frank Downie (under careful supervision of the tram driver), made one final journey between the burgh boundaries at Yoker and Dalmuir. Shortly afterwards, between May and August 1963, the opportunity was taken to lift the tram lines and replace all the cobbles with a new tarmac surface. In this view of Dumbarton Road, the photographer is standing approximately outside the Town Hall, looking towards Clydebank Cross, where a tar-laying machine is operating. To lessen traffic disruption, the contractors are working on the centre of the road, leaving two narrow lanes on either side for through traffic. The greater change, however, as previously noted, was the demolition of all the tenement properties seen here on the left. Between 1980 and 1985, as part of a scheme of environmental improvements, the SDA spent £5 million on further upgrading both Glasgow Road and Dumbarton Road.

This 1930s' view, taken from the foot of Kilbowie Road looking north, shows a Corporation tram alongside the old Clydebank Labour Exchange. As a consequence of the withdrawal of the tram service to Radnor Park and Duntocher in 1949, the tramlines on Kilbowie Road were lifted around 1953. In the late 1970s, despite the failure to proceed with Phase 3 of the proposed Clydeside Expressway, several of the buildings on Kilbowie Road which would have been affected, were demolished anyway. These included both corner tenements at the Cross. Amongst the businesses affected was T.F. Ross's public house, seen here to on the extreme right (from around 1955 this pub was known as the Seven Seas). In its place a new-build public house, known as Chandler's, was opened in December 1981. Also demolished was the three-storey tenement block to the left, with new-build offices later erected on the site. In contrast the tenements on the right-hand side of the road, apart from those above the public house, survived demolition and were later stone-cleaned and renovated. Also still standing is the former Glasgow, Yoker & Clydebank Railway bridge, which nowadays carries trains on the Clydebank Central line.

If any photograph demonstrates the huge change in Clydebank's recent landscape, it must surely be this one! Taken in the early 1970s from underneath the Kilbowie Road Station bridge (now demolished), it shows the Kilbowie Road/Alexander Street/Chalmers Street area prior to the construction of Phase 1 of the Clyde Shopping Centre. At that time all the properties seen here between Alexander Street (first opening on the left) and Chalmers Street (second opening on the left, beyond the old West United Free Church and the Methodist Church) were demolished. Today, where these properties once stood is the rear of Phase 1 of the Shopping Centre (with its service road enclosed within a low brick boundary wall). On the opposite corner of Chalmers Street, where once stood the old Electricity Board showroom and the adjacent Post Office, there is now a new build which includes a bookmaker's shop and the John Brown nightclub (the latter opening in March 2000). On the opposite side of Kilbowie Road, at the corner of Rosebery Street, is the entrance to Rosebery Place (bottom right of the photograph). Immediately beyond this, but out of picture, is a modern office development which was erected on the site of the Blitz-damaged Clydebank Public School.

In this late 1950s' photograph the Lanarkshire & Dunbartonshire Railway Company's Kilbowie Road Station can clearly be seen. From its opening in 1896 until its closure and subsequent demolition in 1977, the station was a predominant fixture on Kilbowie Road. Its island platform was accessed from Kilbowie Road (the entrance is seen here, under the railway bridge) and included a booking office at street level. In October 1906 a handsome granite drinking fountain was erected by the Clydebank Co-operative Society to celebrate their semi-jubilee. Unfortunately, it was destroyed during the Clydebank Blitz and by the time this photograph was taken a flower bed had been laid near where the fountain once stood. For a period from the early 1960s onwards a Christmas tree bedecked with fairy lights was erected annually at the flower bed. Also visible in the photograph are the Rosebery Place tenement (extreme left), the Singer Clock, six tall chimneys within the Singer factory, and on the extreme right the gable end of the Singer Buildings at Binnie Place. From 1980 until the end of 2017 the site of the station and the Rosebery Place tenement was part landscaped and part occupied by custom-built council offices (seen in the recent photograph), but at the time of writing these were being demolished.

Originally a wooden bascule bridge carried Kilbowie Road across the Forth & Clyde Canal and while this was often crowded with Singer factory workers travelling on foot, it was an obstacle to the extension of the Corporation tramway service northwards up to and beyond Radnor Park. The need for a replacement for the bascule bridge proved to be one of the most contentious issues in the lifetime of the former burgh council. Whilst the three interested parties – Clydebank Burgh Council, Glasgow Corporation and the Canal operators – were in general agreement about the need for a more substantial structure, the apportionment of costs was not resolved until 1916. The resulting metal swing bridge, seen here in the 1960s, was constructed by the Brandon Bridge Building Company of Motherwell. By this time the tramlines on Kilbowie Road had been lifted and the road re-surfaced, although the tramlines on the bridge itself remained.

By the beginning of the 1970s, when this photograph was taken, the swing bridge had been removed, following the closure of the canal in January 1963. At that time the canal was partially infilled between here and Linnvale, in preparation for the construction of the new Clyde Shopping Centre; the bridge itself was replaced with a drowned culvert. In the centre of the photograph can be seen the old power station which was demolished in the autumn of 1971. To its left is the new power station, officially opened in November 1971, but demolished after the closure of the Singer factory in 1980. The entire site was re-developed with the construction of Clydebank Business Park, some buildings of which can be glimpsed beyond the former Patio Hotel (now the Southern Cross care home) to the left of the more recent photograph. In 2002 the re-opening of the Forth & Clyde Canal occasioned another significant change: to allow the passage of boats the canal was deepened along its entire length and at the point where it is crossed by Kilbowie Road the surrounding level was raised and the concrete bridge shown below was built.

By 1906, when this view of Singer's Kilbowie Factory was taken, the layout of the factory had taken on a settled look which would largely remain unchanged until modernisation in the early 1960s. The latter largely involved the demolition of the Main Block, seen here in the centre of the photograph. In its place the American owners erected a new single-storey High Volume Domestic building which was officially opened on 23 November 1964. Sadly, however, this had also necessitated the demolition of the Singer Clock. Thereafter, the factory layout remained more or less unchanged until its final closure in 1980. Following this the 86-acre site was bought by the SDA to enable the construction of Clydebank Business Park. At that stage all of the factory buildings were demolished and modern business units were constructed in their place. In addition the site was extensively landscaped and new access roads were laid out circling the site. In the modern view, taken from a site overlooking the business park, some of these new business units can be seen. In the middle distance, sticking out above the surrounding landscape, is the Titan Crane, one of the very few structures to escape the clearance of the Clydebank Shipyard.

In this 1970s' photograph (taken from the Bannerman Street flats) can be seen parts of the old Singer Factory to the east of the Main Building. After the closure of the factory all of these buildings were demolished and the site cleared. Prominent in this view are the rows of single-storey buildings that housed the Printing Department. This produced sewing machine manuals and advertising materials in a multitude of languages. These buildings were the last to be demolished. The stone wall at the extreme bottom right marks the site of Singer Station and the North British Railway line. Today the site is occupied by Clydebank Business Park.

At the turn of the 19th Century several blocks of four-storey tenements were erected on and behind Kilbowie Road, just to the south of Montrose Street. The L-shaped building, seen here around 1907, was known as Bannerman Place. Between this and the railway line (the parapet of the railway bridge can actually be seen in the extreme right-hand corner of the photograph) was Bannerman Street, which led to two further blocks of tenements. In 1971 all of these properties were compulsorily purchased and eventually demolished. Today the site of the old tenements is occupied by council housing built in 1975, which was further extended (under the aegis of the Clydebank Housing Association) in 1985. The metal railings running off to the right in the present-day view mark the western boundary of the old Singer Lye – a series of railway sidings used when Singer workers travelled to and from the factory. Initially, the station on this line was located within this area, but it was later relocated to the other side of Kilbowie Road, where it remains today. Since the station was first opened in 1858 it has been modernised on several occasions, notably when the line was electrified for the introduction of the blue trains.

In this view of The Hill looking south towards the John Brown shipyard, the Blitz-ravaged waste ground on the right, and the absence of tramlines, are strong indicators that the photograph was taken in the 1950s. None of the buildings seen here have survived. All of the Bannerman Place and Bannerman Street tenements (centre left) and those on Montrose Street (first entrance on the left) were demolished in the early 1980s. Those further down Kilbowie Road, from Graham Street to the canal, are also gone, as is the Singer Terrace tenement opposite. Similarly, the Singer factory (seen here on the right) has been demolished. Today, the Atlantis Bar (which opened in March 1962 and is still in business) occupies the corner site which is screened by billboards in the 1950s' photograph, while housing (built in the 1960s) occupies the waste ground which stood opposite.

This view shows the so-called Holy City in Radnor Park, shortly before annexation into the burgh in 1906. Prior to this, Radnor Park was outwith Clydebank Burgh and therefore not subject to the more stringent building standards operating within the burgh. As a consequence the housing shown here was of poor quality and prone to dampness, amongst other problems. The development (seen here from Second Avenue) comprised three parallel rows of flat-roofed terraced housing built primarily to provide affordable accommodation for Singer workers. In contrast, the Radnor Street villas at the extreme top left of the photograph, which were for professional and white-collar workers, were of much better quality. These houses, and the Holy City, were largely destroyed in the Clydebank Blitz. The bandstand in the foreground was part of contractor Robert McAlpine's 'garden city' project. Known locally as 'the better land', the project comprised a mixture of villas and English-style cottages. It was built to the west of the Holy City and largely escaped the devastation of the Blitz. The bandstand itself was eventually demolished, although the houses built on the site were destroyed during the Blitz. In the present-day scene part of the re-developed Holy City project can be seen from the green of the Radnor Park Bowling Club which was laid out in 1907 just to the west of the bandstand. At the first level is Windsor Crescent with, on higher ground, the multi-storey flats on and around Crown Avenue.

The almost whole-scale destruction of the Holy City in March 1941 meant that after the Second World War burgh planners had complete freedom to re-design the area. Surprisingly, as this 1974 photograph (taken by the then *Clydebank Press* photographer, Fergus Wilson) shows, the new development in some ways bore a strong resemblance to the pre-Blitz housing, with parallel rows of flat-roofed houses predominating, although they were joined by seven tall multi-storey blocks of flats. The use of multi-storey flats had been successfully trialed at Dalmuir around 1919, but thereafter not proceeded with. However, the desperate need for new housing after the Blitz prompted a series of high-rise constructions, both here and in the east end of Clydebank. In May 1959 test bores were conducted to ensure ground conditions could sustain the foundations and site clearance work followed in June. The seven multi-storey flats on Kilbowie Hill were built by the Scottish Special Housing Association (SSHA) and were completed in late 1962, with the first tenants moving in during March 1963. The re-building of The Terraces (as the Holy City housing was now called) followed around 1966. However, despite their newness, like the earlier houses, they also suffered from dampness, so much so that in 1990 the council was in negotiations with Scottish Homes (the then owners) regarding the future of the houses. As a consequence The Terraces were demolished and again re-built. At the time of writing further re-construction of The Terraces is taking place along Second Avenue. In the modern view the re-developed Holy City is seen from Clydebank Business Park.

The origins of Radnor Park date back to 1885 when speculative builders began erecting housing on open fields on the crest of Kilbowie Hill, then known as the Skypes. Some of this housing can be seen here, along with the old Radnor Park United Presbyterian Church on the extreme right-hand side. Initially the housing comprised a mix of small villas and other housing, however later builders (including local contractor Leslie Kirk) erected rows of tenements, some of which can be seen in the photograph. In this view from around 1909 the fast-growing community of Radnor Park is seen from the farmlands of North East Boquhanran, to the west of the Skypes. Today, with the exception of the one house that can be glimpsed Janetta Street on the extreme left of the photograph, all of the older properties seen in the early view have been replaced with a mixture of detached properties and multi-storey flats.

The Public School, Clydebank

Boquhanran School occupied a prominent site at the corner of Janetta Street and Albert Road. In this view the school is seen from Green Street, with Radnor Street running along the front of the photograph while Windsor Street is to the building's rear. The school (which is seen here shortly after its opening in 1906) was built to ease the growing pressure on nearby Radnor Park School. Both schools were destroyed during the Blitz and never rebuilt. The site of Boquhanran School came to be occupied by the playing fields of the old Clydebank High School (which opened in 1947). Later, when that school was demolished, the present Clydebank High School was built on the actual site of the old Boquhanran School, with the school's new playing fields being laid on the site of the old Clydebank High School building. In the present-day photograph the new Clydebank High School is seen from the car park to the rear of the Radnor Park bowling green. In the middle distance, to the right of the photograph, can be seen part of the most recent development of The Terraces, with some of the 1960s' multi-storey flats on the hill behind.

The Hill, looking south towards the Clydebank shipyard, with Crown Avenue on the extreme right. By then the road had been cobbled and tramlines laid for the introduction of the tramway services to Radnor Street. None of the tenements seen here on the right-hand side of Kilbowie Road survived the Blitz, although part of a further tenement block (just out of picture on Crown Avenue) escaped serious damage and was later made sound. However, in the 1960s Blitz-damaged tenements on Crown Avenue were finally demolished and new housing, including the tall multi-storey block (seen on the extreme right of the modern photograph, at the entrance to Crown Avenue) was erected. At the foot of The Hill can be seen Radnor House.

This early 1960s' photograph, taken looking west along Glasgow Road with the entrance to Somerville Street first left, shows a solitary workman employed in the lifting of old tram lines. This particular stretch of roadway has since been upgraded on several occasions and is nowadays divided by a raised central carriageway interspersed with modern metal lighting standards. Remarkably, the buildings on the left-hand side of Glasgow Road/Dumbarton Road are still standing, whereas the properties on the right-hand side were demolished in anticipation of the construction of the Clydeside Expressway. The surviving properties include the Art Deco Woolworth store (just out of picture in this view, but seen in the present-day view at the corner of Wallace Street). Built in 1919, it was converted into the Lucky Break Snooker Club in 1982. The tenements between the snooker club and the Town Hall were renovated in the 1980s by the Wimpey Group, who also converted the ground floor shops onto further flats. The finished project, named Centenary Court, was officially opened by government minister Michael Ancram in 1986.

By May 1963, following the cessation of Clydebank's tramway services, the process of lifting the tram rails throughout the burgh and then re-instating the road surface was in full swing. In this photograph a section of Glasgow Road from approximately Belmont Street to beyond the shipyard gate is being re-surfaced. Although the tenement blocks on both sides of the road are also in the photograph, the two blocks on the right-hand side are the more prominent. Erected in 1873, and known locally as Clydebank Terrace, they were the first tenements to be built in Clydebank. By the time this photograph was taken they were clearly showing their age and were considered to be sub-standard. In the early 1970s a proposal was formulated to create an expressway from Glasgow, which would run through the burgh (from its boundary with Glasgow to Clydebank Cross and thereafter up Kilbowie Road to the boulevard). Although these and other tenements on Glasgow Road were demolished in preparation for the construction work, the route of the Clydeside Expressway was curtailed and ultimately reached no further than Partick. Today, Clydebank Housing Association properties fully occupy the north side of Glasgow Road, while the south side presently lies vacant awaiting further development of the shipyard site.

As this early 1900s' photograph shows, a prime stretch of riverbank between Cart Street and Hall Street was by that time being fully utilized for manufacturing. Over the next 100 years or so it would be used for the manufacture of, successively, ships, oil rigs and gas turbines. Although some of the early buildings seen here were later altered, extended or replaced, the wholesale demolition of all the remaining buildings only occurred in 2001 when, following the withdrawal of Kvaerner Energy from Clydebank, the entire site was acquired by a partnership of Clydeside Regeneration Limited and Clydebank Re-built. To date, the bulk of the re-development has taken place around the eastern corner of the shipyard site at what is now Queens Quay in Cart Street. The first of the new buildings on site, in 2007, was the £32 million West College Scotland (formed by an amalgamation of Clydebank College and the James Watt College in Greenock). In close proximity to the new college now are various modern business pavilions such as Titan Enterprise and Aurora House. In a further development closer to the river, in 2017 the new Clydebank Leisure Centre was opened, replacing the older Playdrome Leisure Centre on nearby Argyll Road. Further enhancements of the site include the provision of a paved riverside walkway (which runs the length of the old shipyard) and the renovated Titan Crane (which provides a bird's eye view of the entire site). A major part of the site still remains undeveloped, although there are presently plans for the construction of approximately 1,200 new houses.

This 1960s' view looking west shows some of the properties on the north side of Glasgow Road. From extreme right to left (and up to Whitecrook Street), these include the old Empire Cinema (behind the wall on the right and at the time lying derelict following a major fire) and a group of buildings which included, amongst others, the Parochial Hall, Blackwood's decorators shop and Clark's grain store, the purpose-built former Trustee Savings Bank offices, and Simeone's Café. Of these, the café was the oldest established, having been on the site since 1910. The youngest is the more modern-looking bank offices, which opened in December 1963 – since the 1980s these have been occupied by insurance brokers J. C. Roxburgh & Co. However, all of the rest of these buildings were demolished in the late 1970s in anticipation of the proposed construction of the Clydeside Expressway. Other casualties of the 1970s' redevelopment included the metal bridge (under which the former Lanarkshire & Dumbartonshire Railway line ran) and the public toilets alongside. Both the parapet of the bridge and the toilets can just be glimpsed between the Kizil Mansions (the turreted, domed building) and the tenements on the extreme left. The only other property of those shown here that survived redevelopment is the Kizil Mansions, which were erected in 1913 and still stand today.

In this further 1960s' view of Glasgow Road, this time looking east, some of the buildings seen in the previous, slightly earlier, view remain. The location of the old Empire Cinema alongside St James's Church can now be seen more clearly. St James's was Clydebank's first permanent church and stood from its opening in 1876 until August 1978, when it was demolished for the Clydeside Expressway. A similar fate befell the tall three-storey tenement on the extreme right although the old British Linen Bank building (sandwiched between the tenements and the church) survives today and, at time of writing, is occupied by T. G. Baker (Sound) Limited. In 1964, prior to redevelopment of this area, the ground to the rear of the buildings shown here was purchased by Clydebank Council to enable the building of the new St Andrew's School. In 2010, following the earlier merger with St Columba's School, the first named school was demolished and the site cleared. Today, due to enhancement and landscaping of the dual carriageway, the school site (undeveloped at the time of writing) is now largely hidden from view in the modern photograph. Similarly hidden from view is new housing which was built on the site of the tenements which stood next to the old bank building.

In 1877 the farmlands of East Barns o' Clyde, which lay to the east of John Brown's Clydebank shipyard, were cleared for the construction of a second shipyard, to be operated by Napier, Shanks & Bell. However, within 21 years the company was obliged to vacate this yard to enable the construction of Clyde Trustees' Clydebank Dock. Occupying a 76-acre site, the dock took seven years to build and was officially opened on 25 April 1907. As this early view clearly demonstrates, the dock was initially very successful. It was equipped with a large generating station, an array of mechanical hoists, and traveling cranes jointly capable of handling sixteen ships simultaneously. By the mid-1940s, however, it was handling less and less tonnage, although it wasn't until 1974 that the possibility of closure was announced. Fortuitously, it was briefly reprieved, to be used for the assembly of oil rig modules. These were assembled on the dockside before being skidded onto barges and towed out to sea. Today, apart from the GATX Terminal oil storage facility to the left of the modern photograph, and the small ship repair facility at its eastern end, the dock is little used.

In this 1960s' view of Glasgow Road taken from South Bank Street, on the extreme left is the former Our Holy Redeemer's Chapel School, erected in 1895. The building was converted to an infants' school (known as the 'baby building') in 1913, when a new annexe known as the 'middle' school was opened in South Bank Street. However, in April 1973 the infants' school burnt down and it was replaced in 1980 with a new Our Holy Redeemer's Primary School in nearby East Barns Street. Next to the school can be seen the Argyll Terrace tenement, with the Scottish Episcopal Church standing alongside. All of the buildings shown in this photograph have now been demolished apart from Argyll Terrace and the church. The latter was scheduled for demolition in the 1970s, but was ultimately retained. However, it has since closed and has been lying derelict for a number of years. A Volvo Service Centre now stands on the site of the primary school and 1980s housing and modern industrial units have replaced the other tenements. In addition, a wide raised central carriageway, planted with trees and shrubs, has been laid on Glasgow Road itself.

Further east on Glasgow Road the corner of Napier Street was occupied by Robert D. Laidlaw's Clydeholm garage and car showroom from 1953 until the early 1980s. Both garage and showroom were then demolished and replaced by a modern filling station (built on vacant ground seen here on the extreme right). When this photograph was taken in 1964, the Blitz-damaged tenement to the rear of the garage was still standing, but it was demolished in the 1970s when the Clydeside Expressway was being planned. Also partially visible, in nearby John Knox Street are Elgin Street School (with its distinctive square-shaped dome) and the castellated flat-roofed United Co-operative Baking Society (UCBS) factory with its tall chimney. The former was opened in March 1898 but was demolished in 1987, after its closure three years earlier. The latter, which opened in December 1903, was closed around 1979, and after lying derelict for a few years was demolished. Today, the filling station (on the extreme right of the modern photograph) remains, but otherwise the surrounding area is now occupied by new industrial units and modern housing developments.

In this early 1970s' photograph Glasgow Road is seen from the corner of Hamilton Street, looking west. Just out of picture on the left is Holm Park, the home of Yoker Athletic Football Club. Further west is the former Gulf filling station (at the time of writing a car wash facility) and the Hamilton Memorial Church. The church (easily recognised by its distinctive spire) opened for worship in December 1884 and was the third church to be built in Clydebank. A later addition was the church hall, erected alongside the church in 1929. In 1974, when the congregation merged with Linnvale Parish Church, the church was declared surplus to requirements and has since been used for various purposes, including providing premises for Deans Blinds and the Day Oot Theatre Company. Since this photograph was taken all the tenements seen here on both sides of Glasgow Road have been demolished, as has the former National Assistance Board offices (seen here just left of the Victoria Bar, which is on the extreme right of the photograph). These single-storey offices, which were opened shortly after the passing of the 1948 National Assistance Act, were erected on the site of the old Shandon Mission Hall, and until 1971 dealt with all requests for National Assistance benefits in the Clydebank area. In the mid-1970s, when new premises were built on Kilbowie Road, these offices were vacated and subsequently demolished. Today, in addition to the landscaping of the central carriageway, a mixture of new housing developments and business units occupy much of this area.

In 1963 Council planners began the process of re-developing the 'east end' of Clydebank burgh, from Hamilton Street (the opening of which is seen here at the Barr's Irn Bru billboard) to the Glasgow boundary at Yoker. This involved the demolition of some of the oldest housing in the burgh, including tenements known as the 'Brickland' (the Irn Bru poster is fixed to one of the tenement gable ends). Also demolished were tenements on Hamilton Street, around Gladstone Place, and erected in their place was a mini shopping centre, comprising a supermarket (presently Farmfoods) and shop units. On the south side of Glasgow Road all of the tenement properties to the east of Holm Park were demolished (with the exception of one solitary tenement at Lyle Place) and a number of small industrial units were erected on the site. Also re-developed was the Clydebank Greyhound racing track at the 'Bowery' and a mix of multi-storey flats were built on the site by Crudens in the mid to late 1960s. These included the three twelve-storey blocks seen in the modern photograph. At the time of writing demolition of these flats was underway.